For T. C., with love

N. D.

For Olivia Isabel Conley and Toby Foster Stubbings

P. B.

CANDLEWICK PRESS

 First U.S. edition 2011. Library of Congress Cataloging-in-Publication Data: Dowson, Nick. North : the amazing story of Arctic migration / Nick Dowson ; illustrated by Patrick Benson. p. cm. ISBN 978-0-7636-5271-5 1. Animal migration—Arctic regions. 2. Migratory animals—Arctic regions. I. Title. QL754.D69 2011 591.56'809113—dc22 2010048131 Printed in Humen, Dongguan, China. This book was typeset in Gill Sans. The illustrations were done in watercolor, pen, and pencil. Candlewick Press, 99 Dover Street, Somerville, Massachusetts, 02144. visit us at www.candlewick.com.
11 12 13 14 15 16 SCP 10 9 8 7 6 5 4 3 2 1

# NORTH

## The Amazing Story of Arctic Migration

by Nick Dowson • illustrated by Patrick Benson

AT THE VERY TOP
OF OUR WORLD
is a huge wild place
called the Arctic.
Here in winter, the sun
sinks away,
blizzards fill the darkness,
and even the seas
freeze deep.

Then the Arctic is like
an icy desert.
Only animals like polar bear
and arctic fox—
with coats of fur to keep
the cold away—
can stay alive.

But when spring comes,
bringing back the sun
with light and warmth,
the Arctic changes.

Across its frozen seas,
tiny algae begin to bloom
on the undersides of ice,
coloring it golden brown,

while, on land, plants creep up
through melting snow,
turning the tundra green.

For now, fox and bear
        search for food alone.
But not for long . . .
        soon visitors will come.

Each year, in spring, many
kinds of animals travel
        to the Arctic.
They come because they know
        there will be lots to eat
and space to feed and breed
        and roam in.

From right across the world,
millions risk everything
to fly, walk, or swim here.

IT IS THE GREATEST
        JOURNEY ON EARTH!

SOME OF THE FIRST TO LEAVE
ON THEIR JOURNEY
are gray whales.
This one is young.

Water slides over her
barnacled head
as she glides through the blue
of a Mexican lagoon—
over crabs and sand,
past boats and other whales,
and out into the cold roll
of the Pacific Ocean.

For eight long weeks,
she'll swim north
without feeding . . .

past Los Angeles,

San Francisco,

Vancouver Island,

Anchorage — and into the Arctic Circle.

Five thousand miles
the gray whales swim,
but these birds travel
    twice as far.

From Antarctica, in March,
at the southern tip of
    the world,
terns are on their way.

Unlike the gray whales,
they feed as they go.
Their sharp eyes see sudden
twists of silver, and they dive.

Above them,
    bigger birds wait.
These jaegers bully terns
    to steal their fish:
bully them all the way
    to the Arctic. . . .

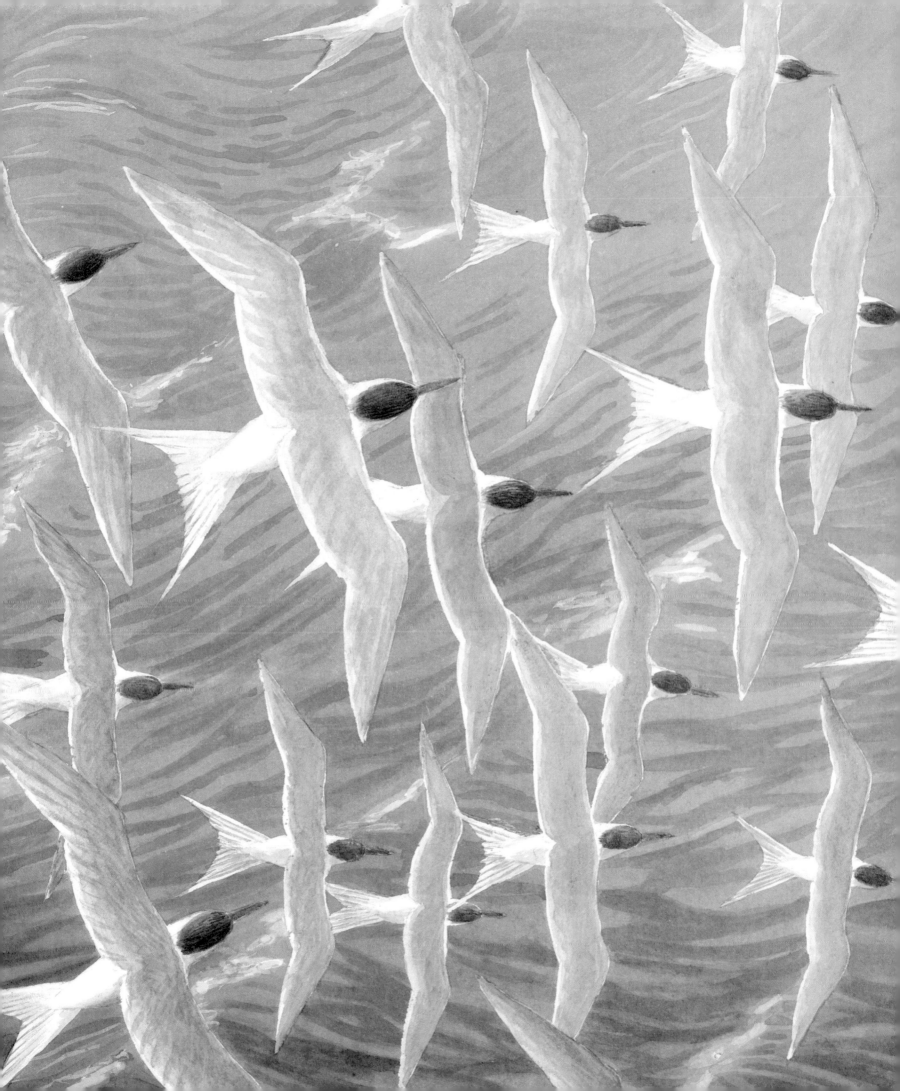

Other birds, too, are getting ready to head north.

Before takeoff, they fuel up to fly.

On a sheltered New Zealand shore, a pair of bar-tailed godwits

sink their bills into the silt, to search for insects, shrimp, and shellfish.

Snow geese grub a stubble field in Mexico

for grains of wasted corn.

At the edge of a Chinese lake, white cranes graze.

Their long legs step like ballerinas'. Their huge bills tear up roots to eat.

Some fly, some swim,
while others walk
    the journey north.

These pregnant caribou
have left the dark
    Canadian forests
where they wintered.

As they trek through
    deep snow
and cross cold,
    swollen rivers,
their coats of hollow hair
keep them warm
    and help them to swim.

Gray wolves slink after them,
    watching for weakness,
hoping a lame one might
    make a meal.

When the herd nears the sea,
four hundred miles
    farther north,
there will be fresh leaves
    and shoots to eat.

Safe on higher ground,
    the caribou will calve.

Not far away,

a month-old Pacific walrus calf

slides after his big, blubbery mother

into the cold April sea.

She'll lead him slowly

up the coast of Alaska,

hungry for shellfish

from the Arctic Ocean's floor.

Smaller swimmers, too,

fill the northern seas.

After spawning, this silver

   herring shoal heads north

to feed on clouds

of blooming plankton.

With bright scales like mirrors,

they swerve together,

fin to fin.

Behind them drift their fry:

trillions of tiny fish

   carried by the current

in the May Norwegian Sea.

And gray-tusked

   narwhal whales,

strange as fairy tales,

join the journey

north to Spitzbergen. . . .

BY LATE MAY, TRAVELERS
CROWD TOGETHER

near the very top of the world,

where even

the coldest frozen seas

are melting.

Ice sheets crack and split,

and bowhead whales

break up the slabs with

their thick, bony skulls.

New sea lanes teem

with creatures

streaming north—

as far as they can go—

to reach their journey's end. . . .

It's summer in
        the Arctic.
All day and night,
the sun spreads light,
warming soil and water.

Tundra flowers
        glow rainbow-bright,
the calm air hums
        with summer bees,
and mosquitoes rise
        like smoke from
        shining pools.

NEW LIFE
        IS EVERYWHERE. . . .

But then September comes.

The days grow shorter.

Sunlight dims and winds begin to blow.

While young terns and goslings,

    cranes and godwits

test their wings, whales and walrus

    are filling up with food.

Soon all the visitors will journey south—

back to where they winter.

Ice stills the sea.
Snow fills the land.
Winter grips the Arctic
    once again.

Now polar bear
    and fox, musk ox
and arctic hare roam
    the frozen night alone.

But not for long. . . .

Always the sun comes

warming back in spring.

And, once more,

around the world,

the wild migration

will begin—

FOR THE GREATEST

JOURNEY ON EARTH!

## About the Arctic

The Arctic is not a continent, but an ocean region that includes thousands of islands and the northern parts of North America, Europe, and Asia.

It is an area of about 5.4 million square miles (14 million square kilometers)—roughly the size of Russia.

The Arctic is the second coldest place on Earth. In winter, the sun never rises and temperatures sink to -40°F (-40°C).

In much of the Arctic, it is too cold and windy for trees to grow, but low-lying flowering plants can survive.

Not many animals can live year round in the Arctic. Those that do include polar bears, arctic foxes, musk oxen, and arctic hares. Each year, in spring, over 180 kinds of animal migrate from other parts of the world and join them.

The ocean closest to the North Pole (where it is coldest) stays permanently frozen. It's called the ice cap.

Recently, global warming has caused the ice cap to start melting, threatening some native Arctic animals with extinction, especially polar bears.

Warmer Arctic seawater also threatens plankton—the main source of food for the birds, whales, and fish that migrate there.

Find out more information about the Arctic online:
www.mnh.si.edu/arctic
www.discoveringthearctic.org.uk

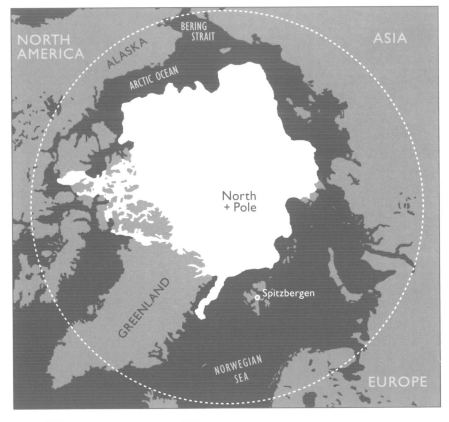

KEY: ☐ Ice cap   ■ Ocean   ■ Land

## Glossary

**algae**—simple plants without roots that grow in sunlit water

**Arctic Circle**—an imaginary line on maps that goes around the Arctic region

**blizzard**—a violent snowstorm with cold, strong winds

**extinction**　when a particular plant or animal dies out forever

**fry**—baby fish hatched from eggs

**global warming**—when the average temperature of the earth rises

**ice sheet**—a giant layer of frozen water

**migration**—when large numbers of animals travel long distances to feed or breed

**plankton**—tiny plants and animals that drift near the surface of the sea

**sea lane**—a path across the sea through melting ice

**silt**—fine grains of mud, sand, and stones that lie at the bottom of oceans or rivers

**spawning**—when fish lay their eggs in water

**tundra**—a treeless plain with soil that stays frozen, except in summer, when enough melts for plants to grow

## Index